WHAT THE HECK IS FILIPINO FOOD?

A BEGINNER'S GUIDE TO FILIPINO COOKING

ADRIAN BRIONES

THIS BOOK IS DEDICATED TO THE RULER OF ALL KITCHENS,

mum

This book is really just a dedication and a thank you to my mum. None of her recipes have been written down, so I thought I'd pen a book to show how much she has taught me. Not only did she teach me how to cook, she also taught me how to clean the house. Seriously! She's like a dust detective – not one speck of dust goes unnoticed. There is no doubt that my mum shaped me into the person I am today – she truly is an inspiration.

Mum was a single parent who worked many jobs to support my brother and I, and yet she still managed to put the most incredible meals on the table without a sweat or sigh. Between you and me, I secretly think that it was therapeutic for her, and I can see why. For me, it's a form of escapism after a busy day at work.

ABOUT ADRIAN...

I was born in San Fernando, which is a town of Pampanga. Pampanga is known as the culinary capital of the Philippines and I have no doubt that my obsession with food lies within my veins. It's a part of me.

After spending so many years in my mum's kitchen, I've come to know the true meaning of food – that there's more to it than just eating it. It must be appreciated and celebrated. Good food should bring about a child-like excitement.

Growing up with food being the main attraction, Mum has always instilled into us that "You are what you eat".

When my brother and I were ill, she would immediately suggest which foods we must eat in order to heal ourselves, and then 15 minutes later a delicious congee would magically appear before us. Food in my family goes beyond the dinner table. Ingredients are put together to create a herbal remedy; when we are stricken with the flu, we combine kumquats, honey, tea and hot water to make an elixir.

Recipe Hunting...

It was quite an adventure writing this book because all the delicious recipes were stored in my mum's genius mind, meaning exact measurements were a challenge. Also, cutting down the number of recipes to include was difficult.

I wish I could have included them all, but it was essential that each recipe be accompanied by a ginormous photo! I didn't want a book full of text with no images homeboy.

Comics & Food...

Judging by the cover, you can probably tell I'm into my comics which somehow tends to blend into my food addiction.

Since I was a kid, I've always dreamed about creating a comic book of my own. I envisioned it to have superheroes fit with different powers from controlling the elements to morphing into any object in sight. Although, I'd end up eating myself as a result of morphing into a cheeseburger or fried chicken! Unfortunately, my illustrative skills never bloomed so when I decided to pen a cookbook, my goal was to somehow, blend both passions – Pinoy food and comics – into one book.

I started my comic book obsession when I was a kid after I grew tired of collecting basketball cards which is why I still appreciate reading from printed paper despite its inevitable extinction and the rise of e-books. Give me a plate full of pork crackling and a stack of my favourite comics and that my friends, would possibly pass as my last meal.

Keep reading and you'll find out just how, in part, this book really came about.

Cooking at home...

The beauty of cooking at home is that you can make as many mistakes as you like without customers sending their plates back complaining that their pork has been overcooked – unless, that is, your house guests do so. I love experimenting with my food and adding some of my bling to the more traditional recipes.

My kitchen experiments started at a young age, from making muffins and other sweet treats to share at school, to selling food outside my house to the bemusement of my neighbours and holding international feast days at work. I got this habit from my mum, who used to make and sell puto seko biscuits on the streets of her village when she was young.

Of course, I've experienced more than my fair share of kitchen failures, but I've always had so much fun doing so. I believe that one must make mistakes to achieve greatness, and so long as you're spending time doing what you love, who cares what others think?

CONTENTS

DEDICATION... 3

ABOUT ADRIAN... 5
    Recipe Hunting / Comics and Food 6
    Cooking at Home 7

INTRODUCING FILIPINO FOOD TO AUSTRALIA... 10

MERIENDA AND DESSERTS...
    Pulled Pork Adobo Pie 14
    Traditional Pinoy Breakfast: Beef Tapa, Rice and Eggs 16
    Homemade Pandesal (Traditional Sweet Bread) 18
    Arascaldo (Chicken Congee) 20
    Green Mango Salad with Sweet Kumquat Dressing 22
    Mama's Banana and Jackfruit Crunchy Fritters 24
    Palitaw (Sticky Rice with Fresh Coconut) 26
    Kamote Que (Candied Sweet Potato) 28
    Frenchy Filipino Toast with Maple Butter 30
    Kalamay (Glutinous Rice Cake) 32

My Country, The Philippines...

    Where I'm From and How I Grew Up   34
    The Humour and The Pork   36

Ingredients From The Garden...   40

Larger/Main Dishes...

    Chicken and Pork Adobo (our national treasure)   44
    Ginataan na Hipon (Spicy Coconut Cream Prawns)   46
    Inihaw na Isda (BBQ Stuffed Rainbow Trout)   48
    Sabaw Sa Kamatis (Veal Shanks in a Tomato-Based Broth)   50
    Estofado (Sticky Pig's Trotters)   52
    Inasal (Filipino Roast Chicken)   54
    Pork Tocino (Cured Pork)   56
    Pimped Up Chicken Tinola with Lemongrass and Corn (Chicken Soup)   58
    Kare Kare (Oxtail in a Peanut Stew)   60
    Longanisa (Sweet Native Filipino Sausages)   62
    Bistek (Steak with Soy and Kumquat Juice)   64
        67

Glossary...

In Closing...   69

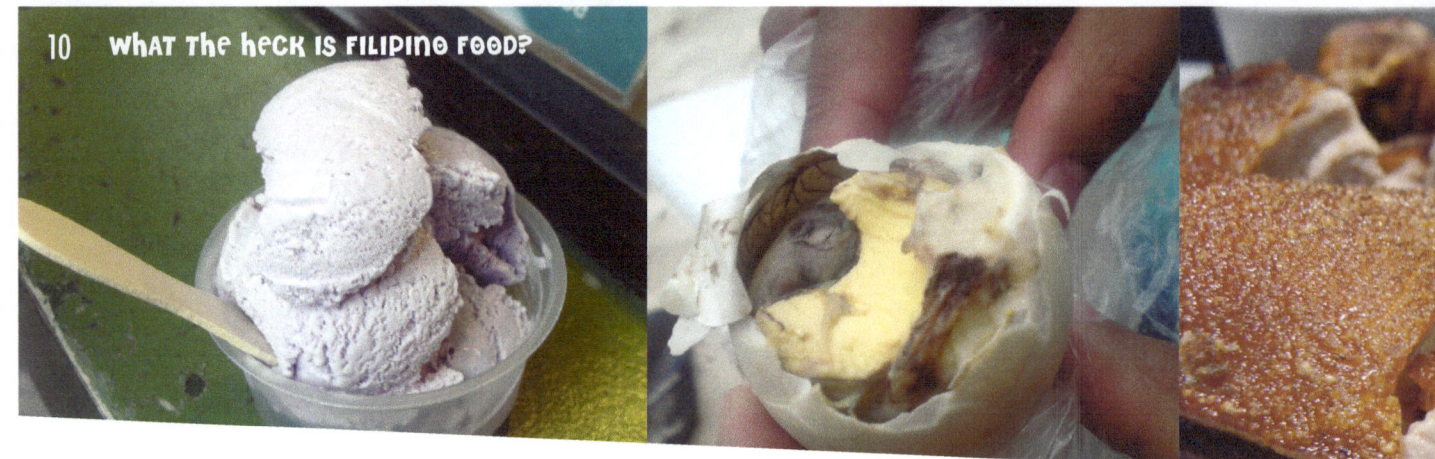

Introducing Filipino Food to Australia...

In no way do I think I'm an expert in this field, far from it in fact, but I think that's the best part. I'm an open book and am always learning to refine my culinary skills. My passion for my country's cuisine became more apparent when I travelled back home last year. I ate things like Coconut Bibingka encased in banana leaves and the infamous Balut (boiled fertilised chicken egg) on the shores of Boracay and Tinapa (smoked fish) from the hawker stalls in the side streets of Manila.

Think of this as my personal take on my culture and a view into how and what I eat everyday.

Every region back home has a different take on each dish, so I wouldn't go as far as to say that these are exactly how the traditional recipes are meant to be cooked. They are an adaptation of my mum's recipes. In fact, many Filipinos (aka Pinoys) may read this book and say, "Hey, that's not how you make that!" Not only did my mum add a few twists to our famed recipes, but so did I! Each generation brings about new innovative variations, taking our dishes into the 21st century whilst respecting the traditions from which they came from.

Each generation brings about new innovative variations

Some examples of other rockin' favourites that I wanted to include were BBQ Pork Skewers, Kuchinta (steamed rice cake), Bibingkang Galapong (coconut rice cake), Pancit Palabok (rice noodles with a golden shrimp sauce) and Singang na Baboy (pork in a

tamarind based soup), but it would have turned this book into an encyclopedia. But not to fret, you can check out my blog for more delicious recipes.

In terms of presentation, Filipino food may not always be the prettiest. But what it lacks in presentation, it surely makes up for in taste. This may or may not be the reason why Filipino food isn't so prevalent in Australia, which is a shame. I truly believe that your taste buds are sorely missing out on this side of Asia's mouth-watering delights.

So, without further adieu, let me introduce an Aussie boy's take on Filipino cuisine...

Merienda and Desserts....
Snacks and the sweet stuff (because I eat dessert first!)

Pulled Pork Adobo Pie

Filling...

500g pork belly
1 teaspoon salt
4 tablespoons sugar
1 teaspoon black pepper
Canola oil
½ cup of soy sauce
4 cloves garlic, crushed
1 onion, sliced
2 tablespoons of white vinegar
1 egg yolk
1 teaspoon double cream
4 bay leaves
4 sheets of butter shortcrust pastry

for best results, leave to thaw in the fridge overnight

To Prepare The Meat...

1. Wash the pork then rub in 1 teaspoon of salt, 2 teaspoons of sugar.

Egg Wash...

2. Combine the egg yolk with the double cream.

To Cook...

3. Slice the pork belly into casserole sized pieces and set aside.
4. Add canola oil to a hot saucepan on medium heat then cook the garlic and onion until golden brown
5. Add the pork belly. We don't want to fully cook it through at this stage.
6. Add the soy sauce, vinegar, salt, sugar, bay leaves and black pepper
7. Simmer for approximately 30 minutes until it thickens, gently stirring occasionally tasting as you go. You may want to add more sugar or salt depending on your taste.
8. Remove the meat from the gravy and place on a cutting board. Using two forks, gently pull the meat apart using a scraping action until you end up with a mix of chunky and finely cut meat (see picture (a).
9. Fill the pastry-lined pie tins with meat and enough gravy. Place a pastry lid on top of each and press the pastry ends together. Trim off any excess.
10. Brush with the egg wash, including the rims, to ensure a golden exterior. Bake for 35-40 minutes at 180°C. Yea baby!

There's Pulled Pork Pie and there's Pulled Pork Adobo Pie. To be blunt, I created this recipe because I ran out of rice – yes, how very un-Asian of me, right? The AFL Grand Finals were on that weekend and it would've been very un-Australian of me not to eat a meat pie during the footy so I thought, why not make a pie out of it? And the rest is history.

I did have to make a few adjustments to the traditional Adobo recipe to make the filling more gravy-like though.

TO LINE THE PIE TINS: You can opt to make your own shortcrust pastry, but like many others, I'm time poor! You also need to take into consideration the time it takes to make the Pork Adobo filling. Using individual pie tins, place a tin face down on a sheet of pastry and cut around the perimeter to form the pie lid. To make the base, repeat, cutting roughly 2 cm out from the tin. Gently lay a pastry base into each pie tin.

TRADITIONAL PINOY BREAKFAST:
Beef Tapa, Rice and Eggs

I grew up eating rice, eggs and Ulam (meaning main) one day and then bacon, eggs and toast the next. My breakfasts went from East to West, which kept my young taste buds dancing.

One of the most classic and traditional Filipino breakfasts is Beef Tapa. The intense soy and garlic flavours combined with a yolky fried egg gives you a good reason to wake up in the morning homeboy!

Ingredients...

½ kg skirt steak
4 cloves garlic
¼ cup dark soy sauce
3 tablespoons raw sugar
1 lemon wedge
Canola oil
1 bowl steamed rice
1 egg

To Marinade The Meat...

1. Slice each piece of meat horizontally to make two equal-sized flat pieces and set aside in a bowl.
2. Crush 2 cloves of garlic and add to the bowl along with the dark soy sauce, raw sugar and a squeeze of lemon juice. Marinade in the fridge for at least 2 days.

To Cook...

3. Add canola oil to a hot frying pan set on medium heat, then add two pieces of steak at a time and cook for 5 minutes on each side. Before flipping over, mop up the marinade with each piece, using a pair of tongs, to give the meat a deep, slightly charred colour. This also saves you from heavy cleaning afterwards! :)
4. Repeat until all the meat is cooked. Set aside. The meat can be covered with foil to keep it warm if desired.

Garlic Fried Rice...

5. Add canola oil to a clean frying pan on medium heat. Add 2 cloves of crushed garlic and fry gently until brown.
6. Add the steamed rice and fry, stirring, until you get bits of burnt rice (they're the best bits!).
7. Fry the egg in a separate pan.
8. Plate up the rice, meat and egg with a side of Green Mango Salad!

ON THE SIDE: Green Mango Salad

homemade pandesal
(traditional sweet bread)

Ingredients...

6 tablespoons melted butter
1 egg yolk at room temperature
¼ cup warm milk
2 cups warm water
2 teaspoons salt
3 teaspoons active dry yeast
⅓ cup white sugar
4 cups all purpose flour
1 tablespoon baking powder
Dried breadcrumbs

To Prepare...

1. Add the melted butter, egg yolk, milk, warm water, salt, yeast and sugar to a large mixing bowl and stir the ingredients from the centre outwards using a wooden spoon. Next add the flour and baking powder and, when mixed, remove the dough from the bowl and knead into a smooth ball.

2. To allow the dough to rise, place it back in the bowl, cover with cling wrap and leave for at least 3 hours at room temperature.

3. Preheat the oven to 180°C degrees.

4. On a floured surface, roll the dough into two thick logs and coat each with breadcrumbs.

5. Slice each log into 2.5 cm thick pieces and lay them flat on baking paper.

6. Sprinkle more breadcrumbs over each piece and bake for 25 minutes or until golden brown.

No Filipino breakfast is complete without the much loved Pandesal smothered in butter. It's slightly sweet, distinctively coated in breadcrumbs and smells like heaven.

Introduced in the 16th Century, Pandesal takes the humble bread roll to a whole new level.

ARASCALDO (Chicken Congee)

Ingredients...

1 whole ginger root, medium in size
1 spring onion
6 cloves garlic
1 cup jasmine rice
⅓ cup glutinous rice
⅓ cup canola oil
1 whole chicken (skin on!)
2 teaspoons salt
2 teaspoons pepper
A handful of kumquats
Spring onions

To serve
Fish sauce
1 egg (optional)

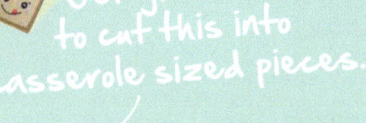 Get your butcher to cut this into casserole sized pieces.

ON THE SIDE: Fish sauce

To Cook...

1. Thinly slice the ginger and spring onion and mince the garlic then set aside on the chopping board.
2. Wash the jasmine rice and glutinous rice twice and set aside.
3. Heat a large pot on medium heat, add the canola oil and fry the ginger and garlic.
4. Drop in the chicken pieces and gently stir until there are no signs of blood and the chicken starts to colour with its juices flowing. Add the salt and pepper.
5. Add the jasmine rice and glutinous rice along with 1 litre of water.
6. Gently stir the ingredients (try to keep the chicken skin intact) then reduce the heat and simmer until the rice is cooked.
7. When serving, add a squeeze of kumquat juice, crack the egg on top and fold the congee over it and garnish with finely chopped spring onions.

I'd describe Arascaldo as our version of Congee. It's packed full of ginger and garlic, and the chicken stock that forms the base is made from scratch.

Back at the old house, during the winter months, I used to plomp myself down by the stairway which had the main ducted heating vent and gobble this down whilst catching up on the latest X-men comics.

Don't forget to add a few squeezes of kumquat juice at the end – it's not the same without it.

Green Mango Salad with Sweet Kumquat Dressing

Ingredients...

1 green mango
1 ripened tomato
4 kumquats
1 teaspoon olive oil
2 tablespoons sugar
Salt

5 mint leaves to garnish

To Prepare...

1. Wash and roughly slice the green mango. You don't need to be exact with the thickness or the length.
2. Dice the tomato and set aside in a bowl.
3. To make the dressing, squeeze the juice of 4 kumquats into a small bowl and add the olive oil, sugar and a sprinkle of salt and combine with the mango and tomatoes.
4. Plate it up with the mint leaves as a garnish.

Back home, unripened mangoes are celebrated as much as ripe mangoes. Though they are quite hard to come by here in Australia, ask your local Asian grocer if they have any in stock.

Hugely popular with Bagoong, a fermented shrimp paste, they also serve as a great pairing with tomatoes in a luscious summer salad.

MAMA'S BANANA AND JACKFRUIT CRUNCHY FRITTERS

I was contemplating whether I should include a banana fritter recipe. I mean, most Asian cookbooks would already have this, right? But (big BUT...) I go crazy over the combination of banana and jackfruit and I know you'll love making this at home.

At family parties, everyone queues up for this. Don't forget to serve it with a big bowl of vanilla ice cream mama!

INGREDIENTS...

4 ripened bananas
12 spring roll wrapping sheets
1 tin of jackfruit
½ cup raw sugar
Canola oil

Vanilla ice cream to serve

TO PREPARE...

1. Cut the bananas into three thin slices.
2. Peel off a sheet of spring roll wrapper and place a slice of banana horizontally across the middle. Lay two pieces of jackfruit on top and sprinkle with a teaspoon of sugar then wrap, folding the two sides from right to left, then rolling gently from bottom to top. Repeat until all the fritters are made, then coat each one with raw sugar.
3. Heat a pan on high heat and add enough oil to deep fry the fritters. Once the oil is hot, carefully drop the fritters in one by one and cook until they start to caramelise. Allow them to cool for at least 5 minutes before eating as the jackfruit will be piping hot!
4. Serve with vanilla ice cream.

PALITAW
(STICKY RICE WITH FRESH COCONUT)

Grate a fresh coconut. I use an old skool grater like we use in the Philippines but any grater would do. Palitaw must be eaten with freshly grated coconut, not packeted desiccated coconut. It not only adds freshness, aroma and texture but eating it should transport you straight to a tropical island.

>  I like to toast the sesame seeds to bring out their full flavour. Add ¼ cup of sesame seeds to a hot pan and cook for no more than 3 minutes, then set aside.

One of the first desserts mum taught me how to make was Palitaw. Not only is it addictive, it's also fun to make. I love watching the glutinous rice rise to the top of the boiling water when it's cooked and grating some fresh coconut on an old skool grater that dates back generations.

INGREDIENTS...

1 cup glutinous rice powder
165 ml coconut milk (a small can)

To serve
1 fresh coconut
¼ cup toasted sesame seeds
White sugar
Vanilla ice cream

TO PREPARE...

1. Add the glutinous rice powder to a large mixing bowl. Gradually drip the coconut milk in as you work the mixture into a dough. It will seem like you need to add more coconut milk but stay patient – it will come together eventually. Once the full can of coconut milk has been added, keep kneading until you end up with a smooth ball, then set aside.

2. Bring 500 ml of water to the boil in a saucepan. Break off 4 cm x 4 cm pieces of dough, roll them in your hands to make small balls, then flatten.

3. Carefully drop 4 pieces of dough at a time into the boiling water. This will help you time the cooking process ... they should rise to the surface at the same time when cooked. They are quite delicate so use either a wooden spoon or chopsticks to remove them from the pan. Lie them flat, not touching, on a plate. Repeat until all the pieces are cooked.

4. Serve immediately while still warm. Put the grated coconut, sesame seeds and sugar in individual piles on a large plate. Dip both sides of each piece in the coconut and sesame seeds then sprinkle with sugar. You can prepare them all before serving, or your guests may prefer to dip their own, eating as they go.

ON THE SIDE: Vanilla ice cream

Kamote Que
(Candied Sweet Potato)

Ingredients...

2 purple sweet potatoes
Canola oil
½ cup raw sugar

To Prepare...

1. Wash the unpeeled potatoes and slice into thin pieces.
2. Heat up a frying pan and add enough oil to shallow fry them.
3. Carefully place the pieces in the pan, cooking in two batches to ensure even cooking.
4. When golden, remove excess oil using a strainer then return the potatoes to the pan.
5. On low heat, sprinkle the raw sugar over the potato pieces. Toss and turn them for even coverage until they are caramelised. The outer edges should be crisp, the centre fluffy, the core candied.

Who knew that you can have the best of both worlds? Fluffy-on-the-inside potatoes covered in a thin crisp glaze. Think candied potatoes!

So easy to prepare and a killer party starter. Make sure you make a second batch though – after the first bite, you'll see why.

This dish represents my childhood years – eating Kamote Que whilst playing the Nintendo. Does the red mushroom in the picture look familiar? Hint: Super Mario Bros.

Frenchy Filipino Toast with Maple Butter

This recipe came about by accident.

Thinking I had some sliced bread stocked away in the freezer, it was not to be. In my fridge however was some leftover Pandesal so I thought, what the heck, let's give this a try.

More than several slices later, I found myself loving the thicker and fluffier texture that standard sliced bread can't provide. Top this off with a slather of butter and pure maple syrup and you too will become a Frenchy Filipino Toast addict!

INGREDIENTS...

3 eggs *preferably free range so the yolk is more likely to be bright orange*
1 tablespoon full cream milk or melted vanilla ice cream
1 teaspoon salt
2 pandesal rolls *see recipe on page 18*
125g butter

Maple syrup to serve

TO MAKE MAPLE BUTTER...

1. Soften the butter by popping it in the microwave for 10 secconds, add the maple syrup and stir in. Set aside in the fridge to cool.

TO COOK...

2. Scramble the 3 eggs in a bowl (large enough to cater for the 2 rolls) and stir in the milk or melted ice cream and salt. The reason I use ice cream is purely for its creaminess, sweetness and vanilla flavour. Stir well to combine. No sugar is required as pandesal is already sweet.
3. Slice the pandesal rolls in half.
4. Heat a pan on medium heat and smother with butter. I usually chuck in 125g but if you care about your health, a thin layer would do.
5. Get dirty and, using your hands, place one slice at a time into the bowl of egg to let each side soak up the egg mixture.
6. Place the coated pieces onto the hot buttered pan, giving each side roughly 2 minutes or until a golden brown is achieved.
7. To serve, top with butter and pure maple syrup or maple butter.

KALAMAY
(GLUTINOUS RICE CAKE)

One thing I always looked forward to was Merienda time, which is taken from the Spanish word for "snack".

After school I'd run in the door, drop my textbook laden bag and jump onto the kitchen stool to watch in amazement as my mum cooked up a mini feast. I honestly think it was all a ploy to get me on a sugar high so I could finish my homework! Well, it worked...

Ingredients...

4 tins coconut cream
1 kg/a packet glutinous rice
250g palm sugar

To Make the Latic
(Coconut Cream residue Topping)...

1. Add 2 tins of coconut cream to a large pot on low heat. Keep stirring until it turns a golden colour and there are no signs of any lumps. This can take up to 15 minutes. Put it in a small bowl and refrigerate for at least 24 hours.

To Cook...

2. Wash the glutinous rice well and cook in a rice cooker, using enough water to cover it to 2.5 cm above the surface of the rice.

3. Prepare the palm sugar. This will be quite hard, so I usually place it in a plastic bag, take it outside like I'm ready for a fight, and start smashing it on the pavement until it breaks up into little pebble sized chunks.

4. While the rice is cooking, add 2 tins of coconut cream to a large pot on low heat. Heat, stirring, until it turns a golden colour and there are no signs of any lumps. Add the palm sugar to the simmering coconut cream and stir it in.

5. Check on the rice. It's ready when you press the top with your finger and it's dry to the touch. Once the rice is cooked, add it to the coconut cream and set the heat to high. This is the stage when you roll up your sleeves and really get to work! Fold in the rice with a wooden spoon until the coconut cream has dispersed evenly. Don't be tempted to stir too vigorously or mush the rice.

6. Once you start to get some crispy rice bits (which are the best bits), place the rice on a flat tray and let it cool. It will start to firm as it cools.

7. Slice it into either square or diamond shaped pieces and top it off with the latic.

My Country. The Philippines....
Where I'm from and how I grew up...

My country was colonised by Spain for nearly 400 years. As a result, the Spaniards infused their delicious Mediterranean style of cooking into our cuisine. Among my favourite desserts and breads are things like Leche Flan (egg custard), Ensaymada (cheese buns) and Pandesal.

Our cuisine is a blend of western and eastern influences taken from our neighbouring countries, with its heavy use of patis (fish sauce), ginger, tamarind and soy sauce; our staples are rice and noodles.

Migrating to Australia at a young age, I didn't get to experience growing up in my village back home. It's funny how you start to track back to your roots in your adult years. Initially, being brought up in Australia was more to do with 'fitting in', if that makes sense. My brother and I were practically the only Asian students in kindergarten and primary school. I often looked at my classmates' lunches filled with sandwiches and prima juices and compared them to mine, which was made up of, say, rice and longanisa (Filipino sausage). I was often mistakenly thought to be Chinese!

> **MY INFAMOUS LUNCHES WERE THE TALK OF THE PLAYGROUND**

There were also the usual assumptions: that I would be an excellent maths student – I wasn't; or perhaps a great science student – I wasn't. But not letting that get to me, I leveraged off my differences and used it as a strength (which may explain why I ended up in Advertising in my adult years!).

So once I stopped thinking of it as a burden I started to swap lunches with my friends and at an early age, began to educate people about my cuisine. In fact, my infamous lunches were the talk of the playground and my fascination with sandwiches quickly switched to meat pies which was also the main inspiration for the Pulled Pork Adobo pie recipe.

The humour and the pork...

I'd describe Filipino food as Asian soul food. Whilst we do have a variety of healthy foods, a large portion of our cuisine consists of fatty food, or what the cool Americans call soul food – think fried chicken and a whole lotta pork, baby!

In fact, our cuisine is surprisingly popular in the US, particularly in New Jersey and San Francisco, where they even have some of our most iconic chain restaurants such as Jollibe and Goldilocks. Lucky bastards!

If you ask any Filipino, our weakness is pork. And by pork, I mean finding any excuse to hold a party so we can eat lechon (a 25 kg pig on a spit) and then turn the leftovers into a beautiful stew (Lechon Paksiw) to keep the celebrations rolling.

This brings to me to the humourous side of us Pinoys. We like to poke fun at ourselves, from our parents' accents, how we always end up arriving late (we call it 'filo time'), tend to feed our guests rather than offer a simple drink, awkwardly point with our lips, call toothpaste Colgate and unknowingly create excessive acronyms for everything (OA, OOC etc..), to how we like to add hot dogs to our spaghetti (which has been sweetened mind you) and our addiction to tinned meats (Spam, Corned Beef).

Like all Asian countries, our main staple is rice. The main difference is that we don't use chopsticks. Funnily, most baby boomers that I know don't even know how to use chopsticks and would prefer not to use them.

> **We Pinoys like to poke fun at ourselves**

You can spot a Filipino at Yum Cha if they specifically ask for cutlery. Many of our dishes are actually cutlery free and are best eaten with your hands. There's even a technique for eating with your hands, one that has been crafted since I was a child and later mastered in my teen years. You must have the perfect scoop.

"I Can ResIst eveRything

... except temptation"
- Oscar Wilde

Ingredients from the garden...

My family strongly believes in only using the freshest of ingredients and, when possible, we'll grow it ourselves. Everything from spring onions and coriander to parsley and garlic can be found in mum's veggie patch – and will be picked just minutes before we start cooking.

In a way, we are paying tribute to the history of our surroundings. Our place was the first house to be built in the neighbourhood, stretching back more than 100 years when the area used to be acres and acres of farmland and fruit orchards. An apple tree still remains in our backyard.

LARGER/MAIN DISHES....

Chicken or Pork Adobo is a national treasure and is our most internationally recognised dish.

I go ape over my family's recipe that combines both pork and chicken. It has a sticky and soupy texture that will have you licking your lips and running for seconds in no time. It's the sort of dish that is best eaten with your hands on top of a bowl of rice – the real Filipino way.

Chicken and Pork Adobo
(Our National Treasure)

Ingredients...

500g of chicken thighs, de-boned (skin on)
500g pork belly
1 teaspoon salt
4 tablespoons sugar
1 teaspoon of black pepper
Canola oil
1 cup of soy sauce
8 cloves garlic, crushed
1 onion, sliced
¼ cup of white vinegar
4 bay leaves

4 cups steamed white rice to serve

or enough to serve 4 people

ON THE SIDE: Green Mango Salad

To Cook...

1. Slice the pork belly into casserole sized pieces and set aside. Repeat with the chicken.
2. Add canola oil to a hot saucepan on medium heat then cook the garlic and onion until golden brown
3. Add the pork belly and chicken. We don't want to fully cook it through at this stage - cook until the chicken turns white and juices start to come out
4. Add the soy sauce, vinegar, salt, sugar, bay leaves and black pepper
5. Simmer for approximately 30 minutes until it thickens, gently stirring occasionally tasting as you go. You may want to add more sugar or salt depending on your taste.

OPTIONAL: When cooked, add canola oil to a hot frying pan then add the pork and chicken to crisp it up

Coconut cream (ginataan) and tamarind would have to be my two all-time favourite ingredients. This dish is another one that is best eaten with your hands.

The juices from the prawns simmered in coconut cream, garlic and chilli create a creamy rich base that tastes like a cross between a seafood bouillabaisse and a laksa.

Being a pretty lazy kid, I still recall my mum having to peel my prawns. Now, as an adult, I realise that this is the best part – especially sucking the juices from the prawn's head!

Ginataan na Hipon (Spicy Coconut Cream Prawns)

Ingredients...

1 kg prawns (unpeeled)
1 bunch of kangkong (water/river spinach), trimmed
2 tablespoons cooking oil
2 cloves garlic, minced
1 onion, sliced
12 pieces of young jackfruit
1 can (560 ml) coconut cream
½ tablespoon salt
Pinch of ground pepper
2 bird's eye chillies, slightly deseeded and minced

To Cook...

1. Trim the whiskers off the prawns and rinse with cold water, then drain and set aside.
2. Snap off the tender leaves and stems of the kangkong, discarding any tough stems and older, yellowish or damaged leaves, then rinse in cold water and drain.
3. Heat the cooking oil in a pan and sauté the garlic and onion, cooking until the onion is translucent.
4. Add the prawns and young jackfruit and let them cook for a few minutes until the prawns turn a slightly rosy colour.
5. Pour in the coconut cream, bring to the boil then lower the heat and simmer the sauce for 3 minutes.
6. Add the remaining ingredients and stir well. Cover the pan with a lid and let it simmer for about 15 minutes. Add the kangkong just before serving, leaving it at the top of the saucepan to steam.

Using a charcoal grill reveals a depth of flavour that makes anything you cook on it, from vegetables to fish, so incredibly moreish.

In summer we would break out the old-age charcoal grill and start cooking up a feast of eggplant, corn, pork chops and my childhood favourite, Inihaw na Isda stuffed with coriander, chopped tomatoes and spring onions and served with a sprinkling of soy sauce and lemon juice.

Funnily, our backyard emits so much smoke that once, our neighbours thought our house was on fire!

Inihaw na Isda
(BBQ Stuffed Rainbow Trout)

Ingredients...

1 rainbow trout, de-scaled and cleaned
2 tablespoons salt
1 ripened tomato
1 bunch coriander
1 spring onion
1 lemon
Olive oil

Black pepper and dark soy sauce to serve

To Prepare...

1. Wash the trout and pat dry.
2. Using a sharp knife, make a gentle cut along the length of each side of the fish, then rub in some salt – roughly 2 tablespoons.
3. To make room for the stuffing, lay the fish on a flat surface and slice it horizontally three-quarters of the way into the fish belly.
4. To make the stuffing, dice the tomato and chop the coriander and spring onion then place these into a bowl. Add a squeeze of lemon juice and combine.
5. Using your hands, gently start filling the fish belly with the stuffing but don't let it overflow. Optionally, you may choose to sew up the side of the fish to contain the stuffing.
6. Douse each side of the fish with some olive oil and place it over a hot grill for 15 minutes on each side. When cooked, the fish should be a nice orange colour with no signs of pink.
7. Very gently, to avoid any rips to the crisp skin, use a large spatula to lift the fish from the grill plate.
8. Serve with black pepper and a side dish of dark soy sauce combined with a squeeze of lemon.

 This dish is best cooked on a charcoal grill.

SABAW SA KAMATIS
(VEAL SHANKS IN A TOMATO-BASED BROTH)

INGREDIENTS...

1 kg veal shanks
1 clove garlic
1 kg ripened tomatoes
1 white radish
4 tablespoons canola oil
5 cups of water
Salt
1 bunch bok choy

Fish sauce to serve

This dish is native to my province, Pampanga. It isn't widely known and when I was travelling around the Philippines, not many locals actually knew what this dish was.

My mum's recipe uses ripened tomatoes, resulting in a tangy but sweet broth.

There are three soups that I rely on when I'm sick: Sinigang (tamarind based), Chicken Tinola and Sabaw Sa Kamatis.

To Prepare...

1. Wash the meat and set aside.
2. Crush the garlic, dice the tomatoes and slice the white radish into 1 cm pieces.
3. If using a stovetop pressure cooker, put on medium heat and add the canola oil. If you don't have a pressure cooker, the cooking time may be extended to 3 hours on medium heat.
4. Add the garlic and tomatoes and stir until it becomes soupy.
5. Chuck in the veal shanks and toss until all the blood is gone and they become slightly brown.
6. Pour in the water and secure the pressure cooker lid.
7. When you hear the whistling (after approximately 20 minutes) gently remove the lid, salt according to your taste and stir.
8. Finally, wash the bok choy, add it to the soup and place the lid back on to let it steam for 5 minutes.

ON THE SIDE: Fish sauce

ESTOFADO
(STICKY PIG'S TROTTERS)

Someone say PIG?! One thing to note about good food – it ain't always pretty!

Pork Estofado is no exception. But what it lacks in presentation, it more than makes up for in taste. It's sweet, salty and sticky and the meat is so tender, it falls off the bone. Did I mention how enjoyable it is gnawing on the bones? A true carnivore's meal.

INGREDIENTS...

1 pig's leg (use a combination of trotters and meat here, adding up to 2 kg in total)
1 onion
1 clove garlic
Canola oil
½ cup vinegar
½ cup water
1 cup dark soy sauce
5 bay leaves
¼ cup sugar

Steamed rice to serve

The tenderness will depend on the age of the pig so ask your butcher.

TO PREPARE...

1. Wash the pig's leg and cut into casserole sized pieces.
2. Thinly slice the onion and crush the garlic then add to a hot pan with a dash of canola oil. Cook gently until the onion and garlic caramelise and turn golden brown, then set aside.
3. Add the piggy pieces and some canola oil to a saucepan and set the heat to medium-high. Stir fry until there are no signs of blood.
4. Pour in the vinegar, water, soy sauce and bay leaves and reduce the heat to a simmer. This is where the slow cooking magic begins and where the flavours start to infuse into the meat, turning it into one of the sticky wonders of the world!
5. Turn the trotters over occasionally, approximately every 30 minutes. Cooking times will vary depending on the age of the pig, but you will know when it's cooked – the trotters will start to shrivel up and the bones will start separating from the meat. Taste or prick the meat to check that it's tender. At this stage you may want to add some sugar, depending on how sweet you like it.
6. Keep simmering until the liquid starts to reduce and the trotters are sticky in texture.
7. Serve with freshly steamed rice.

INASAL
(FILIPINO ROAST CHICKEN)

Beer and chicken? Who would've thought a combination like that would marry up so well.

A twist on a family favourite, the Filipino roast chicken is bloody tasty – tangy, salty, sweet and fragrant and further complimented by an infusion of lemongrass.

The photo to the right signifies my love for music whilst cooking – the guitar is from a trip to the beautiful Boracay Island where my friends and I feasted on food and live music from dusk till dawn.

Annatto seeds will give the chicken a nice golden brown colour. If you cannot find any, you can rub the chicken with brown sugar to give it a nice charred and sticky sweet skin.

INGREDIENTS...

2 tablespoons canola oil
½ cup annatto seeds
1 kg chicken (whole)
2 cloves garlic, 1 crushed and 1 whole
1 small onion, sliced
1 cup beer or apple cider
1 tablespoon lime juice
3 tablespoons kumquat juice
3 tablespoons brown sugar
Salt/pepper
3 stalks lemongrass, chopped into 10 cm strips
1 whole ginger root, medium in size, sliced

TO PREPARE THE ANNATTO SEED OIL...

1. Add 2 tablespoons of canola oil to a small saucepan on low heat, combine with the seeds and heat for 5 minutes. The oil should turn an orange-red colour. Discard any seeds and set the oil aside to cool.

TO COOK...

2. Wash the chicken under cold water then pat dry and set aside.

3. Crush one clove of garlic and slice the onion then place them in a large sandwich/zip lock bag along with the beer or cider, lime juice and kumquat juice. Give it a good shake and set aside. Alternatively, if you don't have a zip lock bag, use a large bowl and cover with cling wrap.

4. Using your hands, rub the inside of the chicken with 2 tablespoons of brown sugar, 1 tablespoon of salt and a pinch of pepper. Place the chicken into the zip lock bag or bowl, shake or move it around to cover it with the marinade and leave it in the fridge to soak up the marinade for at least 5 hours.

5. Preheat the oven to 180°C and lay the chicken breast down in a roasting pan with a rack. Insert the chopped lemon grass, sliced ginger and whole garlic clove into the cavity of the chicken. Alternatively, you could use any leftover lemongrass in place of the rack. Rub the chicken with salt, pepper and 1 tablespoon of brown sugar then baste with the annatto oil to give it some colour.

6. Roast for 1 hour 20 minutes, turning the chicken over and basting with the annatto oil and its juices every 30 minutes. When cooked, cover with foil and set aside for 10 minutes to allow the juices to settle.

PORK TOCINO (CURED PORK)

INGREDIENTS...

1.2 kg boneless pork shoulder roast
(or pork neck if you prefer less fat)
4 garlic cloves, minced
1 teaspoon black pepper
1 cup pineapple juice
1 cup ketchup
½ cup lemonade
⅓ cup dark soy sauce
2 cups brown sugar
3 tablespoons salt
2 teaspoons Tabasco sauce
1 teaspoon oil

Ask the butcher if he can trim off the top layer of fat/skin to save you from doing so.

TO CURE THE MEAT...

1. Slice the pork lengthwise, cutting it into two halves, then cut into 5 mm thick slices. Rub the minced garlic liberally onto the meat, sprinkle over some black pepper and set aside.

2. Add the pineapple juice, ketchup, lemonade, dark soy sauce (to add depth and colour), brown sugar (to aid caramelisation - and we love it sweet!), salt and Tabasco sauce to a large bowl and, using a large wooden spoon, gently combine all the ingredients, ensuring all the pieces are soaked.

3. Transfer the mix to a large air tight container and refrigerate for 4 days to allow it to properly cure. The meat will tend to absorb the moisture so give it a little shake now and then.

TO COOK THE MEAT...

4. The best way to keep the meat tender and juicy is to cook it in three batches. Add 50 ml of water, the oil and enough marinade to boil off the meat to a pan over medium heat.

5. Bring to the boil and allow the liquid to reduce. This process shouldn't take more than 10 minutes; if it does, you've added too much liquid.

6. Once the liquid is reduced, the meat will start to caramelise. This is the crucial moment – start flipping the pieces of meat around until they all get a chance to slightly char, then remove immediately so the meat doesn't dry out. By the 3rd batch, you will have mastered this process!

Tocino is basically cured meat, and my take, which is a twist on mum's recipe, encompasses the four S's of quintessential Asian cuisine, being sweet, salty, spicy and sour. Each piece of meat is like dynamite, having being cured for days, it freakin explodes with flavour.

Tocino can be cooked in many ways. For instance, in summer, you can charcoal grill it and serve it alongside a crisp salad.

Pimped Up Chicken Tinola with Lemongrass and Corn
(Chicken Soup)

Adding the bok choy during the last stage will ensure it keeps its freshness as it doesn't require much cooking time.

This is the Filipino version of chicken soup. Normally cooked without lemongrass and corn, I've grown to love my mum's version with these added kick-ass ingredients.

The lemongrass produces an aroma fit for a king and the corn brings it an element of sweetness. Plus, who doesn't love biting into a juicy corn cob? I sure do!

Tinola is my family's flu elixir because it's packed with garlic and ginger. Oh, and before I forget, please keep the chicken skin intact – don't be a chicken stripper!

Ingredients...

1 whole chicken (skin on!) *— Get your butcher to cut this into casserole sized pieces.*
4 cloves garlic, crushed
2 tablespoons ginger, sliced
2 stems lemongrass, sliced *— Peel away the tough outer layers to reveal the pale lower section of the stem.*
Oil
4 corn cobs, each cut into 4 pieces
Sayote, aka choko, peeled and sliced into wedges *— The core of the choko is extremely bitter so avoid using this.*
2 tablespoons salt
2 tablespoons fish sauce
1 bunch bok choy

Freshly steamed rice to serve

To Prepare...

1. Cut the chicken into roughly ten pieces (skin intact) and set aside. No need to be all even here.
2. Combine the crushed garlic, sliced ginger and sliced lemongrass in a bowl. Heat a wok on medium heat and add the oil when hot. Add the garlic, ginger and lemongrass to the wok and fry, stirring sporadically, for a few minutes.
3. Carefully drop in the chicken pieces and stir fry until there are no signs of blood, watching as all the juices flow.
4. Add the pieces of corn cob and wedges of choko to the mix.
5. Drop the heat to low and add just enough water to cover and submerge the ingredients, which results in a tastier broth. However, if you intend to serve this the next day, you can add more water.
6. Add the salt and fish sauce and simmer for at least 40 minutes, gently stirring every 10 minutes and tasting as you go. Add more salt and fish sauce if required. This should allow sufficient time for the chicken to create a tasty broth.
7. Wash fresh bok choy, add and simmer for a further 7 minutes before serving with freshly steamed rice.

KARE KARE
(OXTAIL IN A PEANUT STEW)

INGREDIENTS...

8 oxtail pieces
2 cloves garlic, crushed
1 onion, diced
3 tablespoons smooth peanut butter
1 eggplant, sliced into wedges
1 teaspoon sugar
A few teaspoons annatto seed powder
3 tablespoons rice flour
Two handfuls snake beans, chopped to finger length
Salt

Bagoong (fermented shrimp and pork fat paste) and steamed rice to serve

TO PREPARE...

1. Firstly, pan fry the cut-up oxtail pieces with the crushed garlic and diced onion until you can see no visible blood. Ensure that all sides are seared to a golden brown tinge.

2. Put in a pressure cooker and top with enough water to cover the meat. Boil on high heat until tender. This part will take up most of the cooking time. Oxtail tastes amazing when the meat falls off the bone, and is well worth the wait. If you don't have the time to wait around, you can leave it simmering for 1-2 hours whilst you do other important things, like making dessert perhaps!

3. Stir in the smooth peanut butter, eggplant and sugar (I like it a little sweet) and chuck in a few teaspoons of annatto seed powder, which gives it a depth of yellow/orange colour, and the rice flour to help it thicken. You want a sauce that is not too runny like a soup nor overly thick like a paste.

4. Add the snake beans towards the end, preferably just before serving, in order to retain their crunch. I tend to always add my vegetables at the end.

5. Serve with steamed rice, with a side of bagoong as a condiment.

Kare Kare is one of those dishes that you never get tired of. There's nothing like it.

It's best cooked in a pressure cooker for melt-in-your-mouth oxtail, otherwise you can spend hours tenderising the meat. Though shamefully, prior to using a pressure cooker, I used to spend the waiting time shaking my booty to my endless music playlist. Actually, I still do that when no one's looking – though I have been busted by a neighbour! Haha!

I think good music and cooking are intrinsically linked. Don't you?

Longanisa
(Sweet Native Filipino Sausages)

Ingredients...

1 kg pork mince (not lean!)
½ cup raw sugar
6 cloves garlic, minced
1 tablespoon salt
2 tablespoons tomato paste
1 teaspoon brown pepper
Canola oil

Rice to serve

1 chopped tomato, topped with salt, as a side condiment

To Make The Sausages...

1. In a large bowl, combine the pork mince, sugar, minced garlic, salt, tomato paste, vinegar and brown pepper.
2. Mix the ingredients with your hands until evenly combined. Not everyone has a sausage maker so keeping this skinless is faster and, in my opinion, more delicious as the outer layer caramelises and slightly chars into a sweet and sticky-like texture.
3. To cure, grab the largest square container you have and some non-stick baking paper. Roll the mince into finger-sized sausages and lay them on the non-stick paper, stacking them up within the container. Refrigerate for 2 days.

To Cook...

4. Sprinkle raw sugar over each piece
5. On a low-medium heat, add canola oil to a hot pan then cook the sausages until they are slightly charred on each side. They should almost caramelise due to the sugar content.
6. Serve with rice and garnish with chopped coriander.

ON THE SIDE: Diced Tomato

This recipe is the newest addition to the family. We used to buy Longanisa from a local producer but have since started making our own and to our delight, have never looked back. You can probably tell by now that Filipinos have an addiction to all things slightly sweet and Longanisa is no exception.

History says that this humble sausage was influenced by the Spaniards during their occupancy ... think Chorizo.

BISTEK
(STEAK WITH SOY AND KUMQUAT JUICE)

ON THE SIDE: Chili and Green Mango

INGREDIENTS...

1 kg rump steak
½ cup Kikkoman soy sauce
⅓ cup sugar
8 garlic cloves
1 red onion
Canola oil

Fresh coriander and steamed rice to serve

TO MARINADE THE MEAT...

1. Cut the steak into thin (minute) steaks. Combine the dark soy sauce, sugar and 2 cloves of crushed garlic. Add the steak to the marinade and refrigerate in a sealed container overnight.

TO COOK...

2. Heat up a frying pan on medium heat, then add the marinaded steak. No oil is required here, just a few teaspoons of the marinade. Stir fry for a few minutes until there are no signs of blood – this process shouldn't take too long.
3. Remove immediately and set aside the meat and its juices in a container.
4. Slice the onion and 6 cloves of garlic and cook with a dash of canola oil in a separate hot pan on medium heat. Add the remainder of the marinade to the pan and bring to the boil.
5. When the ingredients are boiling, add the steak and cook for no longer than 5 minutes.
6. Serve with fresh coriander and steamed rice.

Bistek is the ultimate weeknight-can't-be-stuffed-cooking meal. I might be going out on a limb by saying this, but this is the Filipino version of stir fry.

It takes less than 15 minutes to prepare, and less than 15 minutes to devour the beautifully tender steak atop a bowl of white fragrant rice.

You can also add some snow peas and baby corn to add more texture and flavour.

Glossary...

Annatto seeds Annatto seeds are used to add a yellow to orange colour to a dish. They have a slightly nutty, sweet and peppery flavour.

Bagoong Fermented shrimp and pork fat paste.

Bok choy Also known as Chinese chard or chinese cabbage. Use the leaves and the young, tender parts of the stems.

Coconut cream Available in tins and cartons.

Coriander Also known as cilantro or Chinese parsley.

Eggplant Also known as aubergine.

Fish sauce Made from the liquid drained from salted, fermented anchovies. Has a strong smell and taste; use sparingly.

Ginger Fresh, green or root ginger. Scrape away the outside skin and grate, chop or slice as required.

Glutinous rice Also called sticky rice or sweet rice, this is a type of short-grained Asian rice that is especially sticky when cooked.

Jackfruit This is available in tins in Asian food shops.

Jasmine rice Also known as Thai fragrant rice, this a long-grain variety of rice that has a nutty aroma.

Kangkong Also known as water or river spinach. It has a sweet, mild flavour and may be eaten raw or lightly cooked.

Kumquat Orange-coloured citrus fruit about the size of walnuts.

Lemongrass Lemongrass is native to the Philippines. It is widely used as a herb in Asian cuisine and has a subtle citrus flavour. To use fresh lemongrass, peel away the tough outer layers to reveal the pale lower section of the stem. Needs to be bruised or chopped before using.

Palm sugar Very fine sugar from the coconut palm. It is sold in cakes, also known as gula jawa, gula melaka and jaggery. Palm sugar can be substituted with brown or black sugar.

Sayote Also known as chayote or choko, it can be eaten both raw and cooked. Raw sayote may be added to salads or salsas, and it is often marinated with lemon or lime juice. When cooked, it is generally lightly cooked to retain its crisp texture. The core of the choko is extremely bitter so avoid using this.

Snake beans Also known as yard long beans or Chinese long beans. They are dark green, thin and long (up to 90 cm), with a slightly sweet flavour and crunchy texture.

Dark soy sauce I always use dark soy sauce, but any will do.

Spring onions Vegetables with small white bulbs and long green leaves. Also known as scallions and green shallots.

Spring roll wrapping sheets These are sold frozen and are available in some supermarkets and in Asian food shops.

Tabasco sauce Made with vinegar, hot red peppers and salt; use sparingly.

White radish Also known as daikon or Chinese radish, this is a mild flavoured, very large, white East Asian radish.

In Closing...

The book was written in the same spirit as my food blog – quirky, at times unconventional and not at all too serious. You know that friend who seems to go a little too ape over food, well, in my inner circle, that happens to be me. I'm not trying to win any photography, cooking or writing competitions either.

My book can either be taken as your kitchen's BFF or just as a coffee table book to help build that burning appetite of yours. Either way, thank you for taking the time to sit down and read my ramblings.

It was a freakin incredible journey putting this book together and so gratifying knowing I did it without the things that come with the backing of a major publishing house like a photographer, project manager, prop designers, marketing, distribution and a budget.

I used my own funds which enabled me to really pour my heart and soul into the book in all aspects from recipe testing, winter photography struggles to late night editing. Thank you to my mum for inspiring me to cook and to my special someone who supports and encourages me unconditionally.

Keep Eating!

Adrian Briones

P.S. Never stand in the way of Filipinos and their pork!

Let me know if you end up cooking any of my recipes!

    www.foodrehab.com.au/thecookbook

    whatisfilipinofood@gmail.com

   www.twitter.com/food_rehab

   www.facebook.com/foodrehab

Written and photographed by: Adrian Briones

Book design by: Cain Cooper   www.cain9ine.com

Front Cover Design: Ricardo Gimenes

National Library of Australia Cataloguing-in-Publication Information:

Author: Briones, Adrian

Title: What the heck is Filipino food? : a beginner's guide to Filipino cooking / written by Adrian Briones ; photography by Adrian Briones.

ISBN: 9780987229212 (hbk.)

Subjects: Cooking, Philippine.

Food–Philippines.

Dewey Number: 641.59599

All Rights Reserved. No part of this book may be reproduced or transmitted in any form by any means, electronic or mechanical, including photocopying, scanning, recording or by any information storage or retrieval system, without prior permission in writing from the publisher. The Australian Copyright Act 1968 (the Act) allows a maximum of one chapter or 10% (per cent) of the book, whichever is greater, to be photocopied by any educational institution for its education purposes provided that the educational institution (or body that administers it) has given a renumeration notice to Copyright Agency Limited (CAL) under the Act.

The author asserts moral right to this work.

Copyright ©2011 Adrian Briones

www.ingramcontent.com/pod-product-compliance
Lightning Source LLC
Chambersburg PA
CBHW042127100426
42812CB00017B/2641